INSIDE ART MOVEMENTS

Cubism

Susie Brooks

COMPASS POINT BOOKS
a capstone imprint

Compass Point Books are published by Capstone,
1710 Roe Crest Drive, North Mankato, Minnesota 56003
www.mycapstone.com

Library of Congress Cataloging-in-Publication Data
Names: Brooks, Susie, author.
Title: Cubism / by Susie Brooks.
Description: North Mankato, Minnesota : Compass Point Books, a Capstone
   imprint, [2020] | Series: Inside art movements | Audience: 9-14. |
   Audience: 4 to 6.
Identifiers: LCCN 2018060762 | ISBN 9780756562366 (hardcover)
Subjects: LCSH: Cubism—Juvenile literature. | Art, Modern—20th
   century—Juvenile literature.
Classification: LCC N6494.C8 B76 2020 | DDC 709.04/032--dc23
LC record available at https://lccn.loc.gov/2018060762)

Editorial credits
Series editor: Julia Bird
Designer: Mo Choy Design Ltd.
Image research: Diana Morris

Image credits:
Front cover. Juan Gris, Landscape at Ceret, 1913, oil on canvas, 92 x 60 cm,
Moderna Museet, Stockholm. Bridgeman Images.1. Juan Gris, Landscape at
Ceret,1913, oil on canvas, 92 x 60 cm, Moderna Museet, Stockholm.
Bridgeman Images. 3. Alexander Archipenko, Médrano II, 1913-14, painted
tin, wood, glass and painted oilcloth, 126.6 x 51.5 x 31.7, Solomon R
Guggenheim Museum, NY. © Estate of the artist/ARS, NY & DACS, London
2018. 4. Pablo Picasso, Table in a Café, (Bottle of Pernod), 1912, oil on canvas,
45.5 x 32.5 cm, Hermitage Museum, St Petersburg. © Sucession Picasso/
DACS, London 2018. .4 x 5 Collection/Superstock. 5. Juan Gris, Landscape at
Ceret, 1913, oil on canvas, 92 x 60 cm, Moderna Museet, Stockholm.
Bridgeman Images. 6t. Canaletto, Grande Canal and San Simeone Piccolo,
c.1740, oil on canvas, 124.5 x 204.6 cm, National Gallery, London. Arte
Images/Superstock. 6b. Camiille Pissarro, Boulevard Montmartre, 1897, oil on
canvas, 54.1 x 65.1 cm, Private Collection. Lefevre Fine Art/Bridgeman
Images. 7. Paul Cézanne, Lake at Annecy, 1896, oil on canvas, 65 x 81 cm,
Courtauld Gallery, London. PD/Wikimedia Commons. 8l. Georges Braque,
1908, photograph, published in "Wild Men of Paris", Architectural Record,
May 1910. 8r. Pablo Picasso, 1908, photograph, published in "Wild Men of
Paris", Architectural Record, May 1910. 9t. Pablo Picasso, Les Demoiselles
d'Avignon, 1907, oil on canvas, 243.9 x 233.7 cm, MOMA, NY. © Sucession
Picasso/DACS, London 2018. 4 x 5 Collection/Superstock. 9b. Georges
Braque, The Viaduct at l'Estaque, 1907, oil on canvas, 65.1 x 80.6 cm,
Minneapolis Institute of Arts. © Estate of Georges Braque/ ADAGP, Paris &
DACS, London 2018. Bridgeman Images. 10. Ngontang mask, W. Africa,
Christies Images/Superstock. 11t. Pablo Picasso, Mother and Child, 1907, oil
on canvas, 81 x 60 cm, Musée Picasso, Paris. © Sucession Picasso/DACS,
London 2018. Bridgeman Images/Superstock. 11b. Joseph Csáky, Head, 1914,
bronze, h 38.5 cm, M.T. Abraham Center. © Estate of artist/ ADAGP, Paris &
DACS, London 2018. CC Wikimedia Commons. 12. Georges Braque, Houses
at l' Éstaque, 1908 oil on canvas, 73 x 59.5 cm, Kunst Museum Bern. © Estate
of Georges Braque/ADAGP, Paris & DACS, London 2018. 13. Paul Cézanne,
View of the Sea at L'Éstaque, 1898, oil on canvas, 100 x 81 cm, Staatliche
Kunsthalle Karlsruhe. freundederkuenste.de/Wikimedia Commons. 14.
Edward Collier, Still Life with a volume of Wither's Emblemes, 1696, oil on
canvas, 83.8 x 107.9 cm, Tate London. 15t. Georges Braque, Still Life with
Violin and Pitcher, 1909-10, oil on canvas, 116.8 x 73.2 cm, Museen Basel. ©
Estate of Georges Braque/ADAGP, Paris & DACS, London 2018 4 x 5
Collection/ Superstock. 15b. Juan Gris, Bottles and Knife, 1912, oil on canvas,
54.6 x 46cm, Kröller-Müller Museum, Otterlo. 16. Pablo Picasso, Portrait of
Daniel-Henry Kahnweiler, 1910, oil on canvas, 100.5 x 73 cm, Art Institute,
Chicago. © Sucession Picasso/DACS, London 2018. Ruddy Gold/age
fotostock/Superstock.17. Daniel-Henry Kahnweiler, c. 1910, photograph. PD/
Wikimedia Commons. 18. Jean Metzinger, Tea Time (Woman with a
Teaspoon), 1911, oil on cardboard, Philadelphia Museum of Art. © Estate of
the artist/ ADAGP, Paris & DACS, London 2018. Bridgeman Images. 19. Albert
Gleizes, Paysage à Meudon, 1911, oil on canvas,146.4 x 114.4 cm, Musée
Nationale d'Art Moderne, Paris. © Estate of the artist/ADAGP, Paris & DACS,
London 2018. 4 x 5 Collection/Superstock. 20. Juan Gris, Study for Houses in
Paris, Place Ravignan, 1911, black chalk and gouache on paper, 42.9 x 31.4 cm,
Metropolitan Museum, NY. Bridgeman Images. 21. Robert Delaunay, Red
Eiffel Tower, 1911-12, oil on canvas, 125 x 90.3 cm, Solomon R Guggenheim
Museum, NY. Bridgeman Images. 22. Georges Braque, Le Portugais, 1911, oil
on canvas, 117 x 81 cm Museen Basel. © Estate of Georges Braque/ ADAGP,
Paris & DACS, London 2018. 4 x 5 Collection/Superstock.23. Pablo Picasso,
Ma Jolie, 1911-12, oil on canvas, 100 x 64.5 cm, MOMA, NY. © Sucession
Picasso/DACS, London 2018. ACME Imagery/Superstock. 24bl. Pablo Picasso,
Still Life with Chair Caning, 1912, oil on oil cloth over canvas edged with rope,
29 x 37 cm, Musée Picasso, Paris. © Sucession Picasso/DACS, London 2018. 4
x 5 Collection/Superstock. 24r. Georges Braque, Fruit Dish and Glass, 1912,
wall paper and gouache and charcoal on paper, 62.9 x 45.7 cm, Metropolitan
Museum, NY. © Estate of Georges Braque/ ADAGP, Paris & DACS, London
2018. 25. Juan Gris, Still Life with Guitar, 1913, oil on canvas, 66 x 100.3 cm,
Metropolitan Museum, NY. PD/CC Wikimedia Commons. 26. Pablo Picasso,
Guitar, 1912, cardboard, wood and string, 76.2 x 52.1 x 19.7 cm, MOMA, NY. ©
Sucession Picasso/DACS, London 2018. 27. Grebo mask from Liberia, painted
wood and fibre, Musée Picasso, Paris. 28. Jacques Villon, Young Girl at the
Piano, 1912, oil on canvas, 129 x 96.4 cm, MOMA, NY. © Estate of the artist/
ADAGP, Paris & DACS, London 2018. 4 x 5 Collection/Superstock. 29t.
Francis Picabia, The Procession, Seville, 1912, oil on canvas, 121.9 x 121.9.
National Gallery of Art, Washington D.C. © Estate of the artist/ ADAGP, Paris
& DACS, London 2018. 29b. Raymond Duchamp-Villon, Maison Cubiste,
1912, photograph of maquette published 1913. PD/Wikimedia Commons. 30.
Marcel Duchamp, Nude Descending a Staircase, 1912, oil on canvas, 147.5 x
89 cm, Philadelphia Museum of Art. © Association Marcel Duchamp/
ADAGP, Paris & DACS, London 2018. Oronoz/Album/Superstock.31.
Jules-Étienne Marey, Flight of Seagulls, 1886, chronophotograph. CC/
Wikimedia Commons. 32.Alexander Archipenko, Woman Walking, 1912,
terracotta, h 67 cm, private collection. © Estate of the artist/ ADAGP, Paris &
DACS, London 2018. 33t. Alexander Archipenko, Médrano II, 1913-14,
painted tin, wood, glass and painted oilcloth, 126.6 x 51.5 x 31.7cm, Solomon
R Guggenheim Museum, NY. © Estate of the artist/ ADAGP, Paris & DACS,
London 2018. 33b. Raymond Duchamp-Villon, The Horse, 1914, bronze, h.150
cm, Musée National d'Art Moderne, Paris. Bridgeman Images. 34. Robert
Delaunay, Homage to Blériot, 1914, tempera on canvas, 250 x 251 cm,
Kunstmuseum Basel. De Agostini/Bridgeman Images. 35t. Michel-Eugene
Chevreul chromatic circle, 1839, Paris Didot. 35b. Sonia Delaunay with friends
in studio, 1924, photograph, Bibliothèque Nationale Paris. 36. Marie
Laurencin, Réunion à la Campagne, Apollinaire et ses Amis, 1909, oil on
canvas, 130 x 194 cm, Musée Picasso, Paris. © Estate of the artist/ ADAGP,
Paris & DACS, London 2018. Oronoz/Album/Superstock. 37. Alice Bailly,
Geneva at Night, 1918, paint, wool, 41 x 58cm, Private Collection. PD/
Wikimedia Commons 38. Umberto Boccioni, Dynamism of a Soccer Player,
1913, oil on canvas, 193.2 x 201 cm, MOMA, NY. A. Burkatovski/Fine Art
Images/Superstock. 39t. Piet Mondrian, Composition with Yellow, Blue and
Red, 1937-42, oil on canvas, 72.9 x 65 cm,Tate St Ives. Oronoz/
Superstock. 39b. Cubist House of the Black Madonna, Prague. Werner
Dieterich/Superstock. 40. Fernand Léger, Soldiers Playing Cards, 1917, oil on
canvas,52.7 x 37.8 cm, Kröller-Müller Museum, Otterlo. © Estate of the artist/
ADAGP, Paris & DACS, London 2018. Peter Horee/Alamy. 41t. Pablo Picasso,
Design for the American Manager in Parade, 1917, photograph, © Sucession
Picasso/DACS, London 2018. 41b. WWI battleship with "Dazzle" camouflage.
World History Archive/Alamy. 42. Albert Gleizes, Woman with Black Glove,
1920, oil on canvas,126 x 100 cm, Private Collection. © Estate of the artist/
ADAGP, Paris & DACS, London 2018. 43t. Juan Gris, Harlequin with Guitar,
1919, oil on canvas, 116 x 89 cm, Private Collection. Oronoz/Album/
Superstock. 43b. Jacques Lipchitz, Harlequin and Clarinet, 1920, sandstone,
h 74 cm, Private Collection. © Estate of the artist/Marlborough Gallery, New
York. Peter Horree/Alamy. 44. Paul Klee, Homage to Picasso, 1914, oil on
cardboard,38 x 30 cm,Private Collection. PD/Wikimedia Commons. 45. Frank
Stella, The Dragon and the Leapfrog Fairy, 1985, mixed media, 304.8 x 350.6 x
90.2 cm, Private Collection. © Frank Stella/ ARS, NY & DACS, London 2018.
Christies Images/Bridgeman Images.

First published in Great Britain in 2018 by Wayland
Copyright © Hodder & Stoughton, 2018

All internet sites appearing in back matter were available and accurate when
this book was sent to press.

Printed and bound in China.
1593

Table of Contents

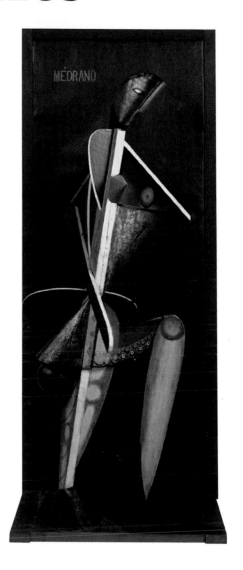

A New View

How do you show the three-dimensional world on a flat, two-dimensional canvas? Is there a way to do this without tricking the eye with an illusion? The cubists wanted to answer these questions—and in doing so, they turned art on its head!

What Is Cubism?

Cubism was an art movement that emerged in the early 1900s in the fast-changing city of Paris. Its leading artists, Pablo Picasso and Georges Braque, felt that painting had reached a dead end. Instead of depicting the world as they saw it, they decided to paint it how they knew it to be. If a bottle looked different from the top or the side, then why not show both views at once!

Table in a Café (Bottle of Pernod), Pablo Picasso, 1912

Abandoning Tradition

The cubists were working in exciting times with modern technology advancing fast. Developments in photography, invented in the 1830s, meant that artists needed to do more than just copy the world. The Impressionists had already made a break from realistic painting—but the cubists went a step further. They rejected perspective, the traditional way of showing space, and celebrated the flatness of the picture surface.

Geometric Shapes

Cubism got its name because the images were packed with geometric shapes. You can see this in Picasso's *Table in a Café* (left), which looks as if it is made from lots of pieces. The objects seem to merge with the background, denying the space they are in. Notice all the different viewpoints—the table is seen from above, the bottle mainly from the side, and so on.

4

Evolving Style

Picasso and Braque inspired other artists, including Juan Gris, Jean Metzinger, Albert Gleizes, and Fernand Léger, to produce their own versions of cubism. The style developed in two phases—first analytic and then synthetic. In synthetic cubism, the artists started using collage, and their work became more colorful. The cubist movement began to disassemble with the outbreak of World War I (1914–1918).

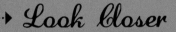

Look Closer

The cubists didn't just use their eyes—they used their memories too. How does this show in the painting by Gris on the right? Think about the way you remember a place—do you have one clear picture or lots of snippets?

Landscape at Céret, Juan Gris, 1913

"Cubism is like standing at a certain point on a mountain and looking around. If you go higher, things will look different; if you go lower, again they will look different. It is a point of view."

Jacques Lipchitz

5

Past Perspective

Before the cubists, most art was representational—in other words, easily recognizable as a landscape, person, or whatever the scene was meant to be. But as the 20th century began, artists became more experimental.

Optical Illusion

Since the 1400s, painters had used a technique called perspective to create the illusion of space on a flat surface. They realized that things in the distance look smaller, paler, and less detailed than anything close up. They identified a point on the horizon, called the vanishing point, that everything recedes toward. This helped them to create an accurate sense of depth, as you can see in this painting by Canaletto.

The Grand Canal with S. Simeone Piccolo, Giovanni Antonio Canal (Canaletto), c.1740

Boulevard Montmartre, Spring Rain, Camille Pissarro, 1897

Quick Impressions

In the second half of the 1800s, the impressionists started to shake up traditional painting. They didn't completely ignore perspective, but they were more interested in capturing the effects of light. Their quick, broken brushstrokes and unmixed colors gave the impression of a fleeting moment. For example, you can sense the passing shower of rain in this scene of Paris by Camille Pissarro.

Simple Shapes

Paul Cézanne was a friend of the impressionists who shared many of their ideas. But instead of painting with small, sketchy brushmarks, he used broader, more deliberate strokes. Cézanne wanted to show the solid side of nature, and to simplify it into basic shapes. He also abandoned the still, single viewpoint, moving his gaze around as he worked.

Geometric Lake

Cézanne said he thought of nature "by means of the cylinder, the sphere, the cone." There are plenty of geometric shapes like these in his lakeside scene below. The cubists loved Cézanne's approach, including the way he played with space. He painted background scenery as boldly as things up close, breaking the rules of perspective.

Lake at Annecy, Paul Cézanne, 1896

Look Closer

Compare the three paintings on these pages. What do you notice about the brushmarks and the use of space? Which artist was most conscious of the flat canvas?

Two Pioneers

"Roped together like mountaineers" was how Braque described his relationship with Picasso! These two revolutionary artists met as young men in Paris where their cubist adventures began.

Braque's Beginnings

By 1907 Georges Braque (a native of France) had been living in Paris for several years. He studied at the official École des Beaux-Arts and soaked up ideas at the city's galleries. Initially dazzled by a contemporary art style known as Fauvism, Braque painted with wild, vivid colors. This began to change when the writer Guillaume Apollinaire introduced him to Pablo Picasso.

Georges Braque

Pablo Picasso

Picasso Arrives

Picasso was a fiery Spaniard who first visited Paris in 1900. A few years later he settled there, setting up a studio in the popular artists' area of Montmartre. In 1907, he made a huge modern painting that sowed the first seeds of cubism. *Les Demoiselles d'Avignon* (top right) shocked Braque when he saw it, but it also inspired him.

A Pivotal Painting

Picasso's *Demoiselles* is a confrontational painting. The naked figures are all flattened up close, while the backdrop jabs toward us in between them. A sharply jagged melon and other fruits perch on an impossibly tilted table in the foreground. Even more unnerving are the monstrous faces of the women on the right, which clearly show the influence of African masks.

Les Demoiselles d'Avignon, Pablo Picasso, 1907

The Viaduct at L'Estaque, Georges Braque, 1907–1908

Sight of Cézanne

Braque painted a nude in response to *Les Demoiselles d'Avignon*, but another event in 1907 inspired him further. There was a major exhibition in Paris showing the work of Paul Cézanne, who had recently died. Braque was fascinated by Cézanne's simplified scenes and his use of shifting viewpoints. He began making paintings like *The Viaduct at L'Estaque* (left), which reveal a clear influence of Cézanne's style.

Look Closer

Braque's painting still has traces of bright fauvist colors, but can you see similarities with Cézanne's work too?

The Influence of Africa

In 1907 Picasso visited an ethnographic museum in Paris and was instantly captivated by what he saw. The African masks and statues there changed his view of art completely and inspired him for the rest of his life.

Art for Impact

Picasso looked at the heavy, simplistic features of the African figures and he realized something. He didn't need to make accurate or decorative images of reality—he could use his art to express something else more powerful and mysterious. The faces on the masks were designed for magical or sacred reasons rather than to look appealing. Picasso began seeing noses, eyes, and mouths as shapes that he could use to make an impact.

New Collections

African art was relatively new to the western world. It began to arrive in the 1870s as Europeans colonized Africa and explored its cultures. Avant-garde artists and their dealers were some of the first people to collect African sculptures. Picasso soon became a keen collector himself.

A ngontang mask, originating from western Africa

Look Closer

Look back to Picasso's *Les Demoiselles d'Avignon*. Can you see similarities with Csáky's sculpture (right) and the mask on this page?

Mother & Child, Pablo Picasso, 1907

Carved Faces

The contrast between African art and western art struck a chord with Picasso. He saw that he could use the former to help him transform the latter. He borrowed the angular noses and almond-shaped eyes that you can see in the mask, and he began making his own faces and figures look like carvings. In paintings such as *Mother & Child* (left), the soft skin and lifelike feel of traditional European art are gone.

Heavy Head

Another cubist artist who looked to Africa was the sculptor Joseph Csáky. He loved the way this so-called "primitive" art didn't copy nature but redefined it. His *Head* is all chunky lines and big, plain surfaces, just like the artifacts in the ethnographic museum. Like Picasso, Csáky realized that he could twist and turn facial features too.

Head, Joseph Csáky, 1914

11

Reduced to Cubes

A collection of houses, as bare as simple building blocks, teeters in a green country valley . . . this painting by Georges Braque of a village in southern France caused outrage when people first saw it!

Houses at L'Estaque, Georges Braque, 1908

Inspiring Scenery

Braque visited Provence in late 1907, freshly inspired by the Cézanne exhibition. The fishing village of L'Estaque was one of Cézanne's favorite places, and Braque sought out the same buildings, bridges, and scenery that his hero had painted repeatedly.

Cézanne's Space

You can easily see the influence of Cézanne in Braque's bold and orderly brushstrokes. Like Cézanne, Braque also avoided perspective and compressed the picture space. This painting is very obviously a painting, not pretending to be a window on the real world. Notice how the trees, roofs, and walls seem to merge in places. This intersection of planes is known as *passage*.

Bare Buildings

While Braque owed a great deal to Cézanne, he also blazed his own trail. He rid his palette of bright Mediterranean color and limited himself to yellow-brown ochres, grays, and greens. His houses have no windows or doors, and their walls don't stand up straight. There is no sign of a sky or horizon, making the space feel all the more tight.

Look Closer

Look back to the Pissarro image on page 6. Do you think Cézanne's painting is closer in style to that or Braque's *Houses at L'Estaque* opposite? Can you see how one approach led to the other?

View of the Sea at L'Estaque, Paul Cézanne, 1898

Critical Name

In 1908 Braque submitted this and some other L'Estaque landscapes to the Salon d'Automne in Paris. The exhibition jury were unimpressed and quickly rejected them all! Later that year Braque held a one-man show where a critic ridiculed him for reducing everything "to cubes." The insult stuck, and in 1909 another critic first used the term *cubism*.

Analytic Vision

By 1908, Picasso and Braque had their new style of painting figured out. They worked in tandem, refining their ideas and pushing boundaries as they analyzed the way we see the world. This phase became known as analytic cubism.

Stripped-Back Scenes

As analytic cubism developed, the style became more extreme. The artists were determined to emphasize the flatness of their canvas while showing how objects really are—how they look different from different sides and angles. They stripped away illusions of 3D space and any bright color that would distract the viewer from the structure of their work.

Still Life

Braque soon moved away from painting landscapes. Instead, he and Picasso turned to another traditional subject—the still life. They loved painting musical instruments, bottles, pipes, pitchers, glasses, newspapers, and other everyday things. Nothing was more satisfying to analyze than the solid, varied, unmoving shapes on a table in front of them.

Still Life with a Volume of Wither's 'Emblemes', Edward Collier, 1696

360 Vision

Look at the silver cup in the corner of this traditional still life. The top of it is oval shaped, just as it would appear in real life. But we know that the top of a cup is round, so our eyes are really being tricked! In Braque's painting (top right of p. 15), the top of the jug is drawn from above, but at the same time the body of the jug is shown from the side. The cubists felt this multi-viewed approach would give us a better understanding of what we see.

Look Closer

Compare a traditional still life with the cubist ones on this page. Which do you think is most effective? Which best sums up the way our eyes are always moving and taking in different aspects of things we see?

"I paint forms as I think them, not as I see them."

Picasso

Still Life with Violin and Pitcher, Georges Braque, 1909–1910

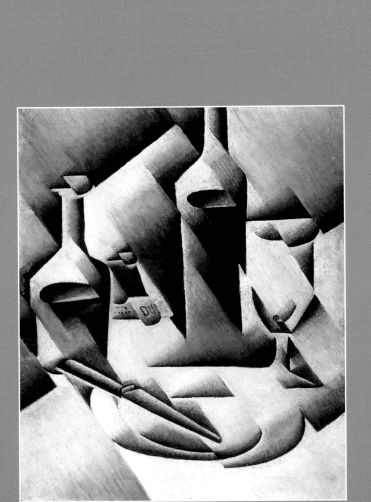

Bottles and Knife, Juan Gris, 1912

Table Turned

Juan Gris was born in Spain but moved to Paris in 1908. He took a studio in the same building as Picasso and soon followed in the cubists' footsteps. In his still life *Bottles and Knife*, everything is reduced to basic shapes and broken into pieces. The high viewpoint of the plate and knife contradicts the side-on bottles, while the table juts upward rather than back. The space around the objects seems as solid as they are— another hallmark of cubism.

In Focus: Fragmented Face

The ghost of a man emerges from a sea of shapes, looking down at his barely there body. His hands are clasped in a traditional portrait pose—but there's nothing else traditional about this painting!

Important Figure

Picasso made this portrait of an important man who helped to launch his career. In its early days, cubism was a difficult style to sell—it was too extreme for people to understand, even in a city bubbling with modern ideas. Then a German art dealer called Daniel-Henry Kahnweiler came along. He was just 23 when he opened his first gallery in Paris.

Portrait of Daniel-Henry Kahnweiler, Pablo Picasso, 1910

An Eye for Cubism

In 1907, Kahnweiler visited Picasso in his studio and saw *Les Demoiselles d'Avignon*. Like Braque, he was both startled and impressed, and the next day he rushed back to buy some preliminary sketches. Before long, Kahnweiler had signed exclusive contracts with Picasso, Braque, and others, showing their work in his gallery. He bought paintings as they produced them, helping to fund their fledgling style.

Shattering Expectations

When Picasso painted Kahnweiler, he demolished everything that people expected from a portrait. Apart from the wave of black hair and the curl of a thin mustache, there are very few clues as to who the subject is. Picasso was actually excellent at drawing and could easily have painted a true likeness. But he wasn't trying to show what Kahnweiler looked like—photographs could do that.

Daniel-Henry Kahnweiler

Jumbled Features

Kahnweiler sat as many as thirty times for Picasso's portrait, waiting patiently as the artist dissolved him into a geometric jumble. Picasso painted him just as he would a still life, combining different views such as the sideways nose and front-on eyes. The head and hands help to give us a focus, while the rest of the figure merges with the room he is in.

▶ Look Closer

Can you make out some details in the painting, including a tie, a watch chain, a wine glass, and an African mask on the wall? What impression do you get of the sitter?

Salle 41

While Picasso and Braque led the way with cubism, it was another group of artists that really brought the style to the public eye. They became known as the Salon Cubists, after the major exhibitions they took part in.

The Salon System

The Salon was the official exhibition of the Académie des Beaux-Arts, and it ruled the Paris art scene for centuries. Its standards were strict and highly conventional, and by the late 1800s, thousands of modern artworks were being refused. Soon rival public exhibitions popped up, including the Salon des Indépendants and the Salon d'Automne. It was at these more progressive shows that the Salon Cubists made their mark.

Getting Noticed

In 1911, a group including Jean Metzinger, Albert Gleizes, Fernand Léger, and Robert Delaunay took over the hanging committee of the Salon des Indépendants. Their aim was to show all their work in one room, and they succeeded in Salle (Room) 41. When the exhibition opened, there was uproar among the public and the press—this cubist style was outrageous! Still, the attention helped to spread the cubist name.

Tea Time (Woman with a Teaspoon), Jean Metzinger, 1911

Look Closer

How does Metzinger's painting here compare to Picasso's *Portrait of Daniel Henry Kahnweiler* on page 16? What are the main differences, and what similarities can you see?

Separate Streams

Picasso and Braque continued to work privately, exhibiting almost exclusively at Kahnweiler's gallery. Some ideas drifted between the two groups, especially via the writer Guillaume Apollinaire, who was friends with them all. But the Salon Cubists maintained their own larger, bolder version of cubism.

Landscape, Albert Gleizes, 1911

Prismatic Paintings

The paintings by Gleizes and Metzinger on these pages are good examples of the Salon style. In comparison to images by Picasso and Braque, their subjects are easier to work out. The Salon Cubists often included people in their pictures, and they weren't so rigorous at stamping out space. These paintings look a bit like prisms, or scenes reflected in broken glass.

Painting Paris

Paris in the early 1900s was the center of the art world. The city was a magnet for creative people, and new developments in technology and society were inspiring everyone, including the cubists.

City of Change

Artists flocked to Paris from abroad, eager to tap into the latest ideas. Cheap rent and a bohemian lifestyle attracted them to areas like Montmartre and Montparnasse. People everywhere were enjoying recent inventions, from the car and telephone to sound recording and cinematography. The cubists' radical way of seeing reflected the modern times.

Look Closer

This sketch at right by Gris shows the site of his and Picasso's studios on the hill of Montmartre. Notice how Gris curved the edges of the buildings. What effect does this have?

Study for *Houses in Paris, Place Ravignan*, Juan Gris, 1911

The Fourth Dimension

Of course, the cubists painted Paris just as they did a portrait or a still life. They delighted in all the geometric shapes around them and looked for every viewpoint they could find. By showing various angles of a building, they could imply a fourth dimension—time. It was like going for a walk around the block without adding seconds to the clock!

Dynamic Tower

From 1889 Parisians discovered a whole new view of their city—from the top of the Eiffel Tower. It was then the tallest building in the world, and the parks and streets below looked small and flat. Robert Delaunay was thrilled by this symbol of the modern age and painted it repeatedly. Here the tower erupts dynamically, almost as if it is alive.

Red Eiffel Tower, Robert Delaunay, 1911 – 1912

Look Closer

What makes Delaunay's painting (above) so dynamic? Look at the lines, shapes, and colors (the Eiffel Tower was painted a deep red until 1892!). How does Delaunay suggest the tower's incredible height? What feeling do you get when you look at this picture?

Who's Who?

Can you make out the subjects of these pictures without looking at the titles? Can you tell who painted each one, or if they are by the same artist? By the end of 1911, Picasso and Braque worked so closely and abstractly that your answers are probably no!

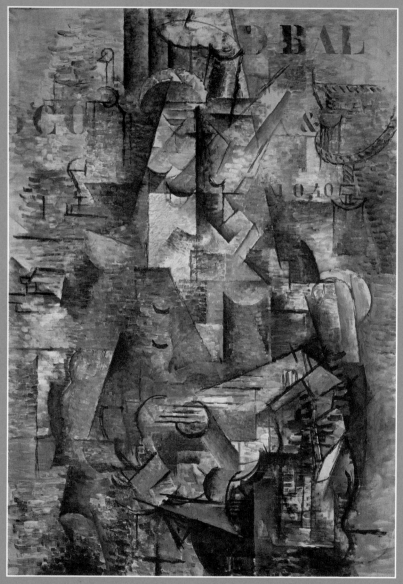

The Portuguese (The Emigrant), Georges Braque, 1911

Starting to Stencil

At this stage, both artists were pushing the limits of analytic cubism. Emphasizing the flat canvas became so important to them that their images began to look like patterns. They also introduced stenciled lettering, something that we know is made on a flat surface. This helped to focus the viewer's mind on the painting itself, not what was being painted.

Portuguese Puzzle

Can you identify the figure in Braque's painting above? You might see an eye, a mustache, a pipe, an elbow and the strings of a guitar. It's a bit like a puzzle— and that's the idea, so we piece together the clues and make our own interpretation of the picture. The cubists liked to challenge their viewers, and in doing so provided a different image for everyone who looked at their work.

Same But Different

Picasso and Braque worked very differently—Braque was slow and methodical, while Picasso was faster, more impulsive. Even so, they interacted so closely that it became difficult to tell their paintings apart. For a while they didn't even sign their canvases to keep their personalities separate from their work. Most evenings they visited each other's studios to look over what they had done during the day.

Ma Jolie (My Pretty Girl), Pablo Picasso, 1911–1912

Musical Medley

Picasso's title *Ma Jolie (My Pretty Girl)* came from a popular song. It was also the artist's nickname for his girlfriend, the subject of this picture. She lurks among all the angular shapes and heavy lines, her fingers strumming a fragmented guitar. As well as painting the letters of the song title, Picasso added a treble clef as a symbol of music.

⤷ *Look Closer*

Can you see differences in the style of these two paintings? Look at the edges of the shapes, how they fill the canvas and how they overlap. Which image is easier to "read?"

Synthetic Shapes

One day in 1912, Braque was walking down a street in Avignon when he noticed a roll of imitation-oak wallpaper in a shop window. He bought some and used it in his first *papier collé*, or paper collage.

The Invention of Collage

Nobody is certain whether it was Braque or Picasso who first invented the collage. They both used the technique at around the same time, in the two pictures on this page. Braque was vacationing with Picasso when he saw the wallpaper, but he waited for his friend to leave before beginning his experiment! He cut up the wallpaper and glued it into a series of charcoal drawings, including *Fruit Dish and Glass* (right).

Still-Life with Chair Caning, Pablo Picasso, 1912

Fruit Dish and Glass, Georges Braque, 1912

Look Closer

The oval shape of Picasso's collage (above) was popular with cubist artists. Why do you think he used it here? Think about the subject of the picture and how it might relate to that.

Everyday Additions

Picasso used printed oilcloth for the chair caning in his collage. He also edged his canvas with rope. The cubists went on to glue newspaper, sawdust, sand, brand labels, sheet music, and more into their work. Suddenly, mass-produced items were finding their way into art, blurring lines between illusion and reality. This use of mixed materials, some imitating others, became known as synthetic cubism.

A Question of Art

The cubists weren't trying to cheat or trick people, but they did raise questions about what could be considered art. By gluing on a fake wood effect, they were removing the need for skill in painting it. This was revolutionary at the time, when high art was an elitist world. Would bringing in ordinary, commercial items somehow make art less special?

Purely Paint

Skill was not a problem for the cubists—in fact, they often painted wood grain or lettering by hand, so it's not always clear what is stuck on and what's not! This work by Gris (below) is a good example, being done entirely in paint with no collage at all. The effect of arranging flat shapes like a jigsaw is typical of synthetic cubism.

Still Life with a Guitar, Juan Gris, 1913

Look Closer

Synthetic cubism became much more colorful than analytic cubism. What other differences do you notice between these images and earlier ones?

25

Picasso's Guitars

A guitar . . . made of cardboard . . . hanging on a wall. No one had seen anything like this in 1912 when Picasso unveiled his model! By turning everyday materials into three-dimensional art, he was taking synthetic cubism to a new level.

Guitar, Pablo Picasso, 1912

3D Collage

Picasso cobbled his guitar together from cardboard, paper, wire, and string. He cut, folded, threaded, and glued, leaving the inside of the instrument open to the outside. The carefully arranged shapes suggest a guitar, without describing it completely. It is simple and geometric, made of flat planes, like a cubist collage exploded into three dimensions.

Redefining Sculpture

Something radical was happening here—Picasso was redefining sculpture. In western art, sculpture meant carving or modeling, using materials such as wood, stone, or clay. Sculptures usually represented people or nature, not items that humans made anyway. Picasso's guitar was an ordinary object recreated using ordinary stuff!

A Grebo mask

Look Closer ◀ ⋯⋯⋯⋯⋯⋯

Picasso had recently bought a mask by the Grebo people of West Africa, similar to the mask on the left. Can you see how this helped to inspire his cardboard guitar? Look at the shapes of the eyes!

La Guitare

When people asked Picasso what his construction was, he apparently replied, "It's nothing, it's la guitare!" For him, the guitar was an obvious subject—an iconic image of Spain, his native country, and also a feast of lines, curves, circles, and other typically cubist shapes. Picasso made collage after collage of guitars around this time. In 1914 he replicated his cardboard model in sheet metal.

Assembling Scrap

Picasso went on to make many more assemblages, as these makeshift sculptures became known. He used scrap wood and metal, upholstery fringing, and other found materials. Later works included a bull's head made from a bike seat and handlebars, a goat with a wicker basket ribcage, and a baboon whose head was built from two toy cars!

The Golden Section

Early cubism was a mystery to the general public, but in 1912 things started to change. Two of the Salon Cubists published a book explaining the movement, and the first groundbreaking cubist exhibition took place.

Gathering in Puteaux

The Salon Cubists regularly met up in a part of Paris called Puteaux, where the artist Jacques Villon had a studio. They called themselves the Section d'Or, or Golden Section, which referred back to mathematical theories from ancient Greece. The group often spoke about math and geometry as they explored possibilities for their art.

A Big Year

In 1912, the Section d'Or artists planned an exciting exhibition. They wanted to show people how cubism had evolved and to help everyone understand their work. In conjunction with the exhibition, Metzinger and Gleizes published *On Cubism*, a book describing the ideas behind the style.

Young Girl at the Piano,
Jacques Villon, 1912

Salon Success

The Salon du Section d'Or of 1912 featured 180 works by 31 artists. Its opening night drew such a large crowd that many guests had to be turned away! The exhibition was a huge success and turned cubism into a recognized avant-garde art movement. Artists including Metzinger, Gleizes, Gris, Léger, Villon (far left), Picabia, and Duchamp were officially on the map.

The Procession, Seville, Francis Picabia, 1912

Look Closer

Compare the paintings by Jacques Villon and Francis Picabia. What feeling do you get from each one? Think about the subjects and the shapes and colors in the pictures. Does the oval frame have an impact on Villon's painting?

Maison Cubiste, 1912

DUCHAMP VILLON.   PROJET D'HOTEL

Maison Cubiste

The 1912 exhibition was timed to directly follow the Salon d'Automne of the same year. This earlier show featured a cubist room, and even a cubist house! Raymond Duchamp-Villon, brother of Jacques Villon and Marcel Duchamp, designed the geometric façade (front). Inside, the house was fully furnished and decorated with cubist paintings.

Speed on the Stairs

There's a mighty clatter as an abstract figure races down a staircase. The title of the painting tells us that the figure is a nude. We can just make out the shape of a person, but most of all we get a feeling of action.

Nude Descending a Staircase, No. 2, Marcel Duchamp, 1912

Capturing Movement

Duchamp conjured up far more noise and energy here than a realistic painting would! He was fascinated by the idea of movement, and how he could show it within the constraints of cubist flattened space. What he really wanted was to stop motion, to pin it down on his canvas. To do this, he repeated shapes so they seem to rattle across the picture from top left to bottom right.

Look Closer

What do you think is cubist about Duchamp's painting? Which elements make it different? Compare it to the futurist work by Boccioni.

Freeze Frames

Look at the photograph below by Jules-Étienne Marey. You can see how images like this had an impact on Duchamp. In the 1870s, both Marey and Eadweard Muybridge made huge leaps in photographing movement. They would capture each stage of a walk, jump, or horse's gallop and show the different stages in series. With every click of a high-speed shutter, a flicker of motion was frozen in time.

Too Dynamic

Duchamp's fellow cubists rejected his dynamic figure for being "too futurist." It did appear at the Section d'Or exhibition of 1912, but the following year something bigger happened. The painting was shown at the New York Armory Show—the first large modern art exhibition in the U.S. It caused an enormous scandal!

Flight of Seagulls, Jules-Étienne Marey, 1887

Scandal in the U.S.

Americans were horrified by Duchamp's treatment of a nude human figure. It was a traditional art subject, but they were used to elegant reclining goddesses, not naked people racing down stairs! One critic described the painting as "an explosion in a shingle factory," as if it looked like shattered stone. Parodies soon sprung up including "Rude" and "Food" descending staircases! Nevertheless, Duchamp's *Nude* is now considered a masterpiece of its time.

3D Cubists

If the cubists were concerned with the relationship between space and the flat canvas, then could their work translate to sculpture? It certainly did in the hands of artists such as Alexander Archipenko, Jacques Lipchitz, and Raymond Duchamp-Villon.

Woman Walking, Alexander Archipenko, 1912

In the Round

Just as cubist painters played with shapes, planes, and shifting viewpoints, so did cubist sculptors. They broke down what they saw, juggled it around, then built it up again. They captured views from different points in space and time, combining them all in one image. A new dimension was added here because a sculpture can itself be seen from any side.

Solid Space

Like cubist painters, the sculptors treated the space around an object as a solid entity. At the same time, they introduced the abstract void in sculpture—a gaping hole in a human figure or other physical thing. Archipenko was one of the first to do this with his *Woman Walking* (left). The body itself is empty, while the emptiness around it is solid!

Dazzling Dancer

Archipenko's *Médrano II* (right) is like a cross between collage and sculpture. Like Picasso's *Guitar*, it is synthetic cubism in 3D form. The flat, bright planes—made of painted wood, metal, glass, and oilcloth—intersect to form the figure of a dancer. Archipenko was exploring movement, perhaps inspired by Marcel Duchamp's *Nude Descending a Staircase*.

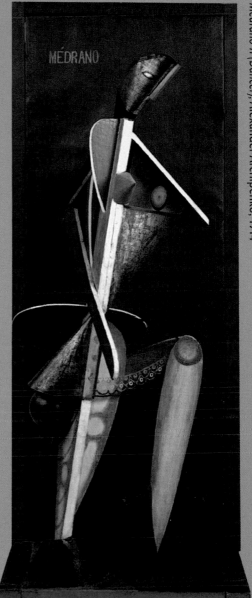

Médrano II (Dancer), Alexander Archipenko, 1914

The Horse, Raymond Duchamp-Villon, 1914

Horsepower

Raymond Duchamp-Villon loved horses and knew all about their grace and power. He was also excited by the new technological age, so when he sculpted *The Horse* (left), he made it part machine! Most of the animal's natural form is taken over by hard edges and mechanical shapes. Duchamp-Villon's work on this was interrupted by World War I (1914–1918), when horses were gradually replaced by armored vehicles on the battlefields.

⟶ *Look Closer*

Duchamp-Villon's sculpture looks dynamic and strong. Can you recognize any features of the horse? Can you see it gathering its hooves, ready for to gallop or jump?

In Focus: Dynamic Rainbows

Whirling propellers in rainbow colors light up the sky over Paris. The Eiffel Tower looks very small from up here in the air! Robert Delaunay painted this kaleidoscopic scene to celebrate the thrill of airplane flight.

Homage to Blériot, Robert Delaunay, 1914

Cross-Channel Flight

The newsflash came on July 25, 1909—Louis Blériot had flown a plane across the English Channel! It was less than six years after the Wright Brothers in the U.S. had launched the first powered aircraft. Blériot's flight, from France to England, won him a prize of over $1,200 and caused a sensation around the world. Delaunay wanted to capture the excitement in paint.

The Age of Aviation

Delaunay's picture above isn't completely true to life—Blériot flew from Calais, not Paris, and he used a monoplane (just visible in the top center of the picture) rather than a biplane like the one shown above the Eiffel Tower. Delaunay was really paying homage to the new age of aviation, as well as the French flying hero.

Flickering Colors

The bright, overlapping discs in Delauney's painting seem to whirl and flicker with energy. The artist used his interest in scientific color theories to achieve this effect. He was fascinated by the way colors affect one another, looking bolder when they're next to their opposites, or complementaries. In the 1800s, the chemist Michel-Eugène Chevreul had devised a color wheel to help explain this idea.

Michel-Eugène Chevreul's color wheel

Look Closer

Can you see links between Chevreul's color wheel and Delaunay's painting? Which of Delaunay's colors zing out most?

Sonia Delaunay (right) in her husband's studio with two friends wearing her fashions.

Orphic Cubism

Another influence for Delaunay was his artist wife Sonia, who made a patchwork quilt for her son's crib in 1911. The intersecting shapes reminded her of cubism and inspired the couple to develop a colorful and abstract version of the style. This became known as orphism for its mysterious quality that didn't always refer to the real world.

Female Cubists

Art was traditionally a very male world, and this was still the case when the cubists began working. But the turn of the 20th century opened doors for female artists, and plenty of talented women made an impression on cubism.

Changing Society

Society in Europe was progressing, bringing new opportunities for all. By the 1900s, women were being accepted into art schools and being allowed to draw from nude models. They were freer to paint in public places and play an active role in exhibitions and café discussions. None of this had been possible just 50 years before.

Women Versus Men

Despite this progress, the traditional view that artists were men lingered. Women received less recognition for their work and tended to be overshadowed by their male peers. They would often depict domestic subjects or veer toward the decorative arts or fashion. For example, Sonia Delaunay became well known for her geometric clothing designs.

Réunion à la Campagne (Apollinaire et ses Amis), Marie Laurencin, 1909. The figures here include Gertrude Stein (far left), Apollinaire (center), Picasso (to Apollinaire's right), and Laurencin herself (far right).

A Feminine Style

Marie Laurencin was an important figure who explored the feminine side of cubism. She was romantically linked with Guillaume Apollinaire and befriended Picasso, Braque, and the Section d'Or group too. Her paintings are full of flowing curves, in contrast to more angular cubist works. The painting below left shows herself and Apollinaire among a group of their friends.

Geneva at Night, Alice Bailly, 1918

The Infamous Gertrude Stein

As captured in Laurencin's group portrait, Gertrude Stein (a writer, not a painter) played a vital part in the cubist movement. She was a wealthy American with a keen eye for modern art, and she built up a famous collection. Stein championed the cubists, especially Picasso and Gris, writing about them and their work. Along with her brother, she held weekly gatherings for avant-garde figures in Paris.

From Switzerland and Spain

The Swiss artist Alice Bailly developed her own version of cubism, using wool to imitate brushstrokes! She sewed yarn onto canvas in multi-colored blocks (above), which look a bit like Cézanne's daubs of paint. Another prominent figure was María Blanchard, a Spaniard and close friend of Juan Gris. Her style was heavily influenced by his work but often more brightly colored.

Cubism Abroad

Even in cubism's early days, the world took notice and reacted. Similar movements sprung up in Italy, Russia, England, the U.S., and as far away as China and South America. The style even inspired architects in Czechoslovakia.

Spreading the Style

Cubism spread to other countries as artists and dealers traveled. Foreigners visited or moved to Paris, both to make and to purchase art. Daniel-Henry Kahnweiler held exhibitions abroad, while his Paris gallery attracted collectors from Germany, Russia, and the U.S. Events like the Armory Show in New York also helped to broadcast the style.

Dynamism of a Soccer Player, Umberto Boccioni, 1913

Fast-moving Futurism

In Italy, a movement called futurism began in 1909, inspired by cubism but more concerned with speed and technology. The futurists embraced the modern world with dynamic images like Umberto Boccioni's *Dynamism of a Soccer Player* (above). A robotic figure, half-man half-machine, powers through space in an explosion of vibrant color. It is more a picture of energy than of the soccer player himself.

International Trends

Futurism caught on in Russia in around 1912. Here it quickly developed into the more industrial style of constructivism, and the abstract, geometric suprematism. In England there was vorticism, a cubist movement emerging in 1914. The Steins helped to introduce cubism to the U.S., where artists used it to reimagine scenes of New York City.

Composition with Yellow, Blue and Red, Piet Mondrian, 1937–1942

Geometric Extremes

The Dutch artist Piet Mondrian visited Paris in 1912 and fell under the influence of Picasso. Back in the Netherlands, he gradually took cubism in his own direction and, along with other artists and designers, developed a style called de stijl. The geometric elements are clear to see in Mondrian's painting at left. Unlike cubism, however, de stijl was based on strict horizontals and verticals.

Look Closer

Czech designers latched onto cubism as a way to modernize their architecture. What cubist features can you see in this building?

Working through War

The most creative phase of cubism took a devastating blow in 1914. World War I (1914–1918) broke out in Europe, dispersing the artists on military service or into exile abroad.

Away to Battle

The cubists called up to fight in the war included Braque, Metzinger, Gleizes, Léger, Villon, and Duchamp-Villon. Some, including Braque, were badly injured, while Duchamp-Villon and the writer Apollinaire lost their lives. As citizens of neutral Spain, Picasso and Gris avoided combat and spent most of the war years in Paris.

Soldiers Playing Cards, Fernand Léger, 1917

The Tubist

Léger painted his *Soldiers Playing Cards* while recovering in Paris from a poison gas attack. He had already made sketches in the trenches, where front-line soldiers like him fought. Here he shows his fellow infantrymen in a moment of relaxation, smoking pipes as they enjoy a game of cards. They look like machines, made up of the trademark cylinders that gave Léger the nickname "the Tubist".

Hostile at Home

The instability of war led people in France to be suspicious of the avant-garde. Cubism was seen by many as a "foreign" or "German" art, partly because it was so popular with German collectors. Germany was the enemy, and immigrants such as Daniel Kahnweiler were driven into exile, losing everything. Picasso and Gris faced hostility too, but like many other artists they continued to work.

Cubist Costumes

One of Picasso's wartime projects was to design sets and costumes for a ballet called *Parade*. This meant traveling to Rome, Italy, where the company, the Ballets Russes, rehearsed. Picasso created huge geometric outfits made of wood, metal, pâpier maché, and other materials. They had the desired effect of making the dancers move stiffly, like robots.

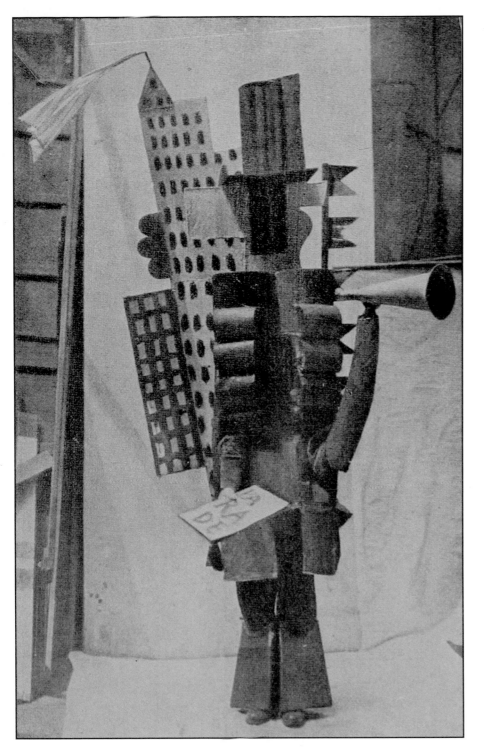

Picasso's design for the costume for the American Manager in *Parade*, 1917

A ship painted in dazzle camouflage

Look Closer

"Dazzle camouflage" was used in World War I (1914–1918) to confuse the enemy by making it difficult to see the outline of a ship or which way it was going. Can you see how designs like this might have been inspired by cubism?

A New Order

World War I (1914–1918) changed society and the way everyone, including artists, viewed the world. It led to a pull back from radical experimentation, and many of the cubists toned down their work or switched to more traditional styles and subjects.

A New Dealer

In the absence of Kahnweiler, another young dealer took the reins of cubism during the war. Léonce Rosenberg signed up Picasso, Braque, Gris, and Léger as well as Metzinger, Gleizes, and others. From the end of 1918—the year the war ended—he staged a series of solo exhibitions for his artists, showing that cubism had survived.

Woman with Black Glove, Albert Gleizes, 1920

Crystal Cubism

Cubism during the late and post-war years looked more restrained and orderly than earlier work. The geometric shapes that the artists favored were bigger and flatter than ever before. You can see this in Gleizes's *Woman with Black Glove*, which feels simple, clear and calm. This pared-down version of the style became known as crystal cubism.

Back to Tradition

Artists started looking back to traditional themes around this time. It was part of a movement called "the return to order," which rejected avant-garde ideas. Many artists, including Picasso for a while, turned to painting realistically, inspired by classical art from ancient Greece and Rome. Characters from 16th-century Italian theater also became popular subjects—especially the trickster Harlequin.

Harlequin with Guitar, Juan Gris, 1919

Harlequin and Clarinet, Jacques Lipchitz, 1920

Harlequin

Gris painted around 40 pictures of Harlequin during the years 1917–1925. In this one above, his character is made of large, interlocking shapes—but Gris also added quirky little details. For example, *Harlequin's* hands double as parts of the guitar and the floor seems to creep toward his feet. You can see hints of the joker's diamond-patterned costume in the zigzag across his shoulders.

Look Closer

Jacques Lipchitz made his *Harlequin* in three dimensions. What similarities can you see between this sculpture and the painting by Gris?

Modern Art Forever

Cubism never really took off again after World War I (1914–1918)—but it had already changed art forever. By challenging the way artists interpret the world around them, the cubists made the first truly modern art.

A New Understanding

Hardly anyone had questioned the way painters show space since the discovery of perspective 500 years earlier! In this move alone, the cubists changed history. But also thanks to them, people had a fresh understanding of art. They realized it could be challenging, unorthodox, even ugly—not necessarily a pretty picture on a wall.

Homage to Picasso, Paul Klee, 1914

The Abstract Path

Cubism needed its viewers to be involved, to fill in the gaps and use their imagination. The cubists didn't abandon the real world as their subject, but they inspired other artists to. Their focus on the picture surface paved the way for abstract art like Paul Klee's *Homage to Picasso* (left). Later artists, from the abstract expressionists to the minimalists, explored this idea in their own ways.

Look Closer

How has Klee paid homage to Picasso in this painting? What makes his work different from cubism? Which type of art do you prefer?

Everyday Assemblages

Working with everyday materials was another breakthrough by the cubists.
It was soon taken up in a World War I movement called Dada, where artists
made collages and used ordinary objects to challenge the boundaries of art.
Assemblages like Picasso's went on to play a part in surrealism and pop art.
More recent artists have made their own cubist-style constructions, like the
one by American Frank Stella below.

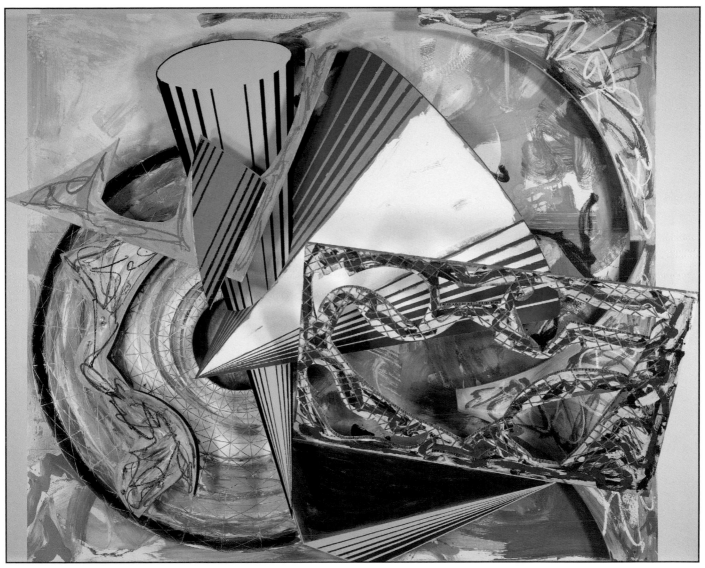

Il Drago e la Cavallina Fatata (The Dragon and the Fairy),
Frank Stella, 1985

Key to the Future

After the cubists had burst onto the art scene, painters and sculptors had a new sense
of freedom. They didn't need to make images that people recognized—they could
break rules and create art for its own sake. This opened up endless opportunities for
the future. Cubism was like a stepping stone for every modern art movement since.

Glossary

abstract—not representing an actual object, place, or living thing

abstract expressionists—a group of American artists (1940s–1950s) who created art for emotional effect, rather than representing something physical

artifact—a human-made object

assemblage—an artwork made from a collection of found or gathered objects

avant-garde—new and experimental

bohemian—an unconventional or free-spirited way of living

canvas—a strong type of fabric that many artists use to paint on

carving—an artwork made by cutting into material such as wood or stone

classical—relating to ancient Greece and Rome

collage—an artwork made by sticking bits of paper, fabric, or other materials onto a surface

complementary colors—colors that have maximum contrast

compress—flatten

constructivism—a Russian movement (1913–1930s) that focused on "constructing" art for the modern age, using abstract geometric shapes and industrial materials

Dada—a European movement (1916–1924) that aimed to destroy traditions in art, with often nonsensical or tongue-in-cheek work

elitist—seemingly superior to others

ethnographic—relating to the study of people and cultures

evolve—develop gradually

exile—when someone is banished from the country they live in

fauvism—an art movement (c.1905–1910) in which artists such as Henri Matisse used extreme colors and fierce brushstrokes

fragmented—broken into pieces

illusion—something that tricks the eye or isn't what it seems

impressionists—a group of French artists (c.1870–1900) who painted outdoors and used broken brushstrokes to capture the fleeting effects of light and the weather

minimalists—extreme abstract artists in the U.S. (1960s–1970s), whose work was based on highly simplified, impersonal shapes

orphism—a short-lived offshoot of cubism (c.1912–1914), which focused on the expressive qualities of color

palette—a board that artists mix their paints on; also used to describe the range of colors in a painting

parody—a funny or exaggerated imitation

passage—patch-like brushwork that blends intersecting planes (flat surfaces in space) together

perspective—the art of showing three-dimensional objects on a flat surface, creating the effect of depth and distance

pop art—an art movement led by artists in the UK and U.S. (1950s–1970s) that drew inspiration from popular culture and commercial imagery

replicate—make an exact copy of something

representational—showing the true physical appearance of things

still life—a painting or drawing of an arrangement of objects, such as fruit in a bowl

studio—an artist's indoor workplace

suprematism—a Russian abstract art style (c.1913–1930) based on simple geometric shapes, painted in limited colors

surrealism—an art movement (1924–1966) that focused on the subconscious mind and the uncanny images of dreams

synthetic—artificially or chemically made, usually to imitate a natural product

unorthodox—different from what is usual, traditional or expected

vorticism—a British art movement (1914–1915) that used hard-edged abstract shapes to express the dynamism of the modern world

Read More

Books
Venezia , Mike. *Pablo Picasso*. Getting to Know the World's Greatest Artists. New York: Children's Press, 2015.

Internet Sites
MoMA Learning: Cubism
www.moma.org/learn/moma_learning/themes/cubism

Tate: All About Cubism
www.tate.org.uk/art/art-terms/c/cubism/all-about-cubism

Tate: Who Is Pablo Picasso?
www.tate.org.uk/kids/explore/who-is/who-pablo-picasso

Timeline

1830s Photography is invented and over the next few decades starts to prompt new experiments in art.

1860s Claude Monet and others develop the Impressionist style.

1870s Eadweard Muybridge and Jules-Étienne Marey develop stop-motion photographs.

1889 The Eiffel Tower opens in Paris.

1890s Paul Cézanne advances his blocky, geometric style that will soon inspire the Cubists.

1895 The Lumière brothers show the first motion picture in a Paris cinema.

1900 Georges Braque moves to Paris.

1903 In the U.S., the Wright brothers achieve the first manned airplane flight.

1904 Pablo Picasso moves to Paris.

1906 Paul Cézanne dies in Provence.

1907 An exhibition of Cézanne's paintings inspires artists in Paris. Braque visits Provence to paint the landscape. Picasso studies African masks and paints *Les Demoiselles d'Avignon*. Daniel-Henry Kahnweiler opens his gallery.

1908 The art critic Louis Vauxcelles uses the word *cubes* to describe Braque's paintings. The phase known as analytic cubism begins.

1909 The art critic Charles Morice is the first to use the term *cubism*. Louis Blériot flies a plane across the English Channel from France. Futurism begins in Italy.

1911 Jean Metzinger, Albert Gleizes, Fernand Léger, and others hang their work in one room at the Salon des Indépendants. They become known as the Salon cubists. Picasso and Braque work together in Céret in the French Pyrenees.

1912 Picasso and Braque both make their first collages. The phase known as synthetic cubism begins. The Salon Cubists hold the successful Salon du Section d'Or exhibition, with an accompanying book called *On Cubism*. Picasso creates his cardboard *Guitar*. Robert and Sonia Delaunay develop Orphism.

1913 The first Armory Show, a modern art exhibition, is held in New York—Marcel Duchamp causes a scandal with his *Nude Descending a Staircase, No. 2*. The constructivist and suprematist styles emerge in Russia.

1914 World War I breaks out. Many artists are conscripted to fight. Kahnweiler is exiled to Switzerland. Cubist-inspired vorticism begins in England.

1915 Braque suffers a severe head injury in the war. The phase known as crystal cubism starts to develop. Scientist Albert Einstein publishes his *General Theory of Relativity*.

1916 The Dada movement begins in Switzerland.

1917 The Dutch style de stijl is founded. Picasso visits Rome to design sets and costumes for the ballet *Parade*.

1918 Raymond Duchamp-Villon dies in a French military hospital. World War I ends.

1918-1919 Léonce Rosenberg holds a series of cubist exhibitions in Paris.

1921 Picasso turns to a more classical style of painting.

1922 A room is devoted to Braque at the Salon d'Automne.

1924 The Surrealist movement is founded.

1937 Picasso paints his cubist-style *Guernica* in response to the Spanish Civil War (1936–1939).

1939 World War II breaks out.

1945 End of World War II.

1961 Braque becomes the first living artist to have his work exhibited at the Louvre in Paris.

1963 Braque dies in Paris.

1964 Sonia Delaunay becomes the first woman to exhibit at the Louvre in her own lifetime.

1973 Picasso dies in southeastern France.

Index